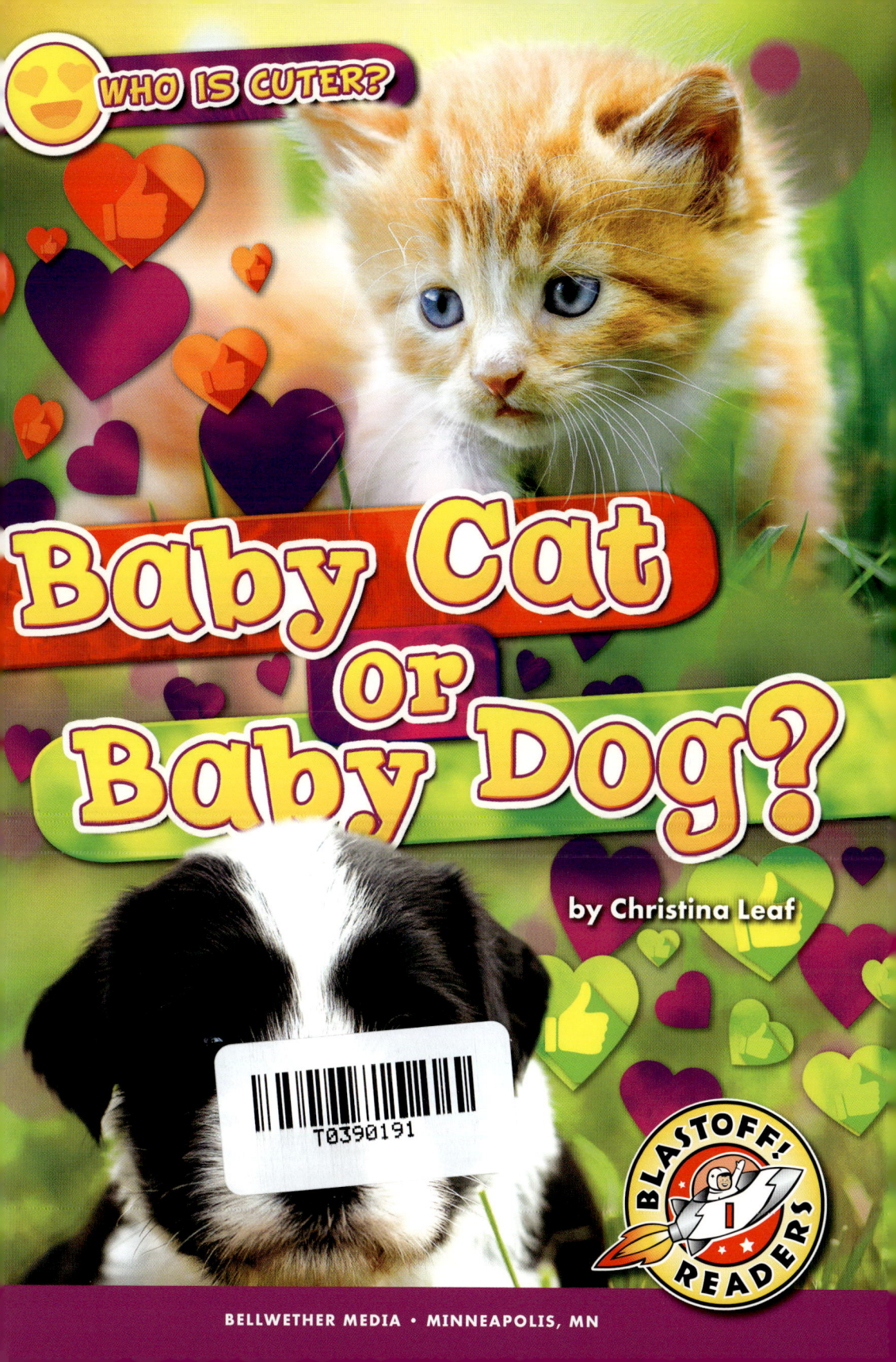

WHO IS CUTER?

Baby Cat or Baby Dog?

by Christina Leaf

BELLWETHER MEDIA · MINNEAPOLIS, MN

Blastoff! Readers are carefully developed by literacy experts to build reading stamina and move students toward fluency by combining standards-based content with developmentally appropriate text.

LEVELS

Level 1 provides the most support through repetition of high-frequency words, light text, predictable sentence patterns, and strong visual support.

Level 2 offers early readers a bit more challenge through varied sentences, increased text load, and text-supportive special features.

Level 3 advances early-fluent readers toward fluency through increased text load, less reliance on photos, advancing concepts, longer sentences, and more complex special features.

★ **Blastoff! Universe**

Reading Level

   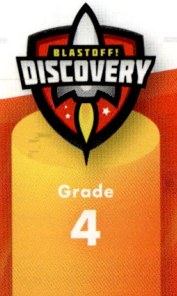

Grade **K**

Grades **1–3**

Grade **4**

This edition first published in 2025 by Bellwether Media, Inc.

No part of this publication may be reproduced in whole or in part without written permission of the publisher. For information regarding permission, write to Bellwether Media, Inc., Attention: Permissions Department, 6012 Blue Circle Drive, Minnetonka, MN 55343.

Library of Congress Cataloging-in-Publication Data

Names: Leaf, Christina, author.
Title: Baby cat or baby dog? / Christina Leaf.
Description: Minneapolis, MN : Bellwether Media, Inc., 2025. | Series: Blastoff! readers: who is cuter? | Includes bibliographical references and index. | Audience: Ages 5-8 | Audience: Grades K-1 | Summary: "Developed by literacy experts for students in kindergarten through grade three, this book introduces the differences between baby cats and baby dogs to young readers through leveled text and related photos"– Provided by publisher.
Identifiers: LCCN 2024003089 (print) | LCCN 2024003090 (ebook) | ISBN 9798886870282 (library binding) | ISBN 9798893041422 (paperback) | ISBN 9781644878729 (ebook)
Subjects: LCSH: Kittens–Juvenile literature. | Puppies–Juvenile literature.
Classification: LCC SF445.7 .L428 2025 (print) | LCC SF445.7 (ebook) | DDC 636.7/07–dc23/eng/20240301
LC record available at https://lccn.loc.gov/2024003089
LC ebook record available at https://lccn.loc.gov/2024003090

Editor: Suzane Nguyen   Designer: Andrea Schneider

Printed in the United States of America, North Mankato, MN.

Table of Contents

Kittens and Puppies!

Cats and dogs are fun pets! Baby cats are called kittens. Baby dogs are puppies!

kittens

puppies

5

These pets can be many colors. Puppies are also many sizes. All are cute!

Noses and Ears

Kittens have small noses. Most puppies have long noses. They are called **snouts**!

snout

Kittens have
pointy ears.
Some puppies do, too.
But other puppies
have rounded,
floppy ears.

**pointy
ears**

Pounce and Fetch

Both babies show big feelings. Kittens purr. Puppies wag their tails!

13

These babies play! Kittens **stalk** and **pounce** on toys. Puppies **fetch** toys and learn tricks!

**fetching
a toy**

**pouncing
on a toy**

15

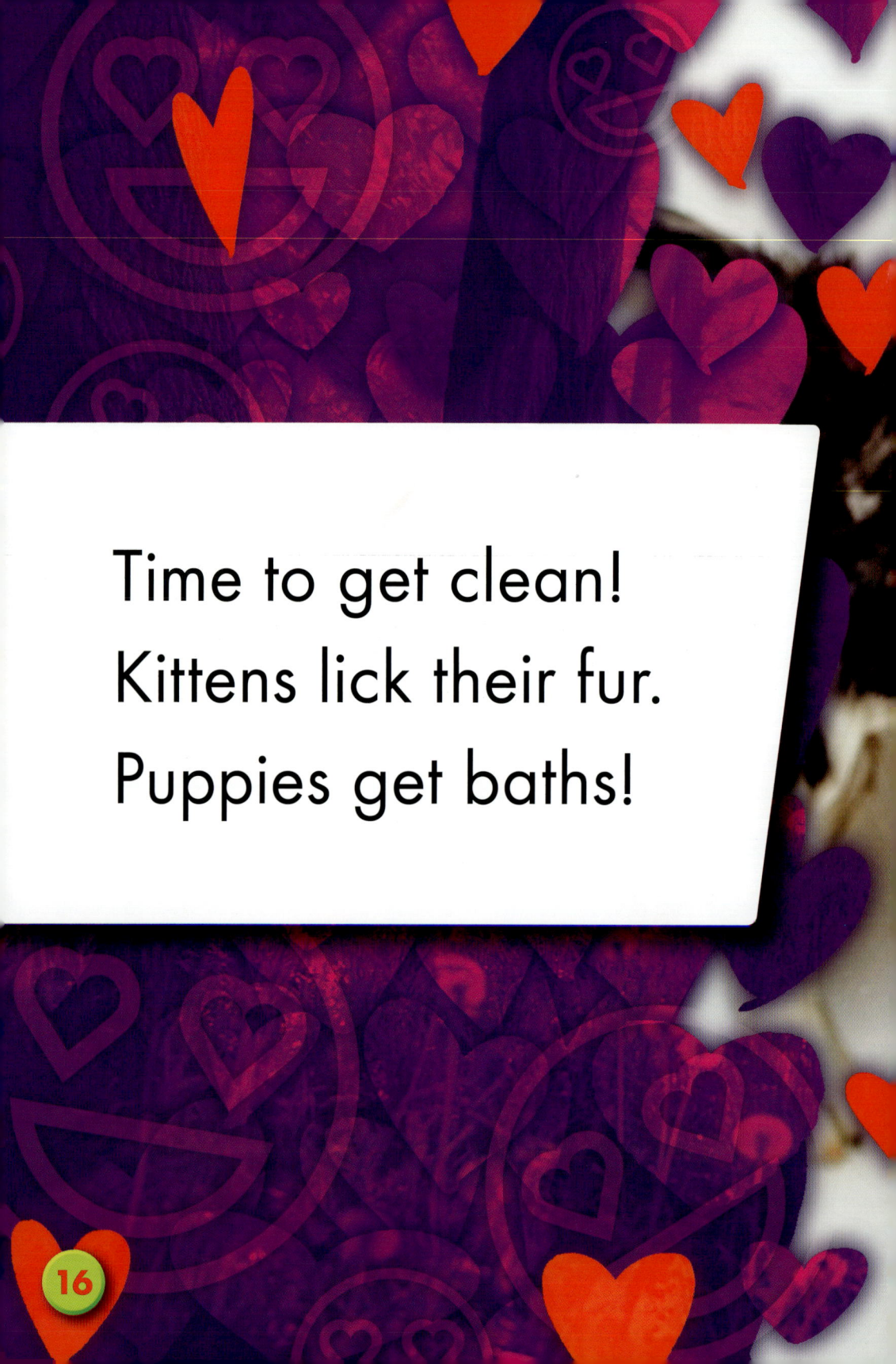

Time to get clean!
Kittens lick their fur.
Puppies get baths!

Kittens say meow.
Puppies say woof!
Which one wins
this cute contest?

Who Is Cuter?

meow

pointy ears

small nose

Baby Cat

purrs

stalks and pounces

licks fur

20

snout →

woof

Who is your pick?
Vote at
BellwetherMedia.com

rounded,
floppy
ears

Baby Dog

wags tail

fetches
and learns
tricks

gets
baths

Glossary

fetch

to go after and bring back

snouts

the noses and mouths of some animals

pounce

to suddenly jump on something

stalk

to follow closely and quietly

To Learn More

AT THE LIBRARY

Cutest Animals on the Planet. Washington, D.C.: National Geographic, 2021.

Leaf, Christina. *Baby Cats*. Minneapolis, Minn.: Bellwether Media, 2022.

Rathburn, Betsy. *Baby Dogs*. Minneapolis, Minn.: Bellwether Media, 2022.

ON THE WEB

FACTSURFER

Factsurfer.com gives you a safe, fun way to find more information.

1. Go to www.factsurfer.com.

2. Enter "baby cat or baby dog" into the search box and click 🔍.

3. Select your book cover to see a list of related content.

Index

The images in this book are reproduced through the courtesy of: jdross/ Adobe Stock, front cover (kitten); tstajduhar, front cover (puppy); Utekhina Anna, p. 3 (kitten); Dorottya Mathe, p. 3 (puppy); JanVlcek, pp. 4-5; Orientgold, p. 5; Zanna Pesnina, pp. 6-7; Vaclav Sebek, p. 7; Damian Pawlos, pp. 8-9; evrymmnt, p. 9; Sergei Ginak, pp. 10-11; Mikayla Nicole Photo, p. 11; Mahlebashieva/ Adobe Stock, pp. 12-13; Roman Pyshchyk, p. 13; eli_asenova, pp. 14-15; mdorottya/ Adobe Stock, p. 15; Andrii Zorii, pp. 16-17; bugra tombak, p. 17; FatCamera, pp. 18-19; PHATSUKE, p. 19; Benjamin Simeneta, p. 20 (kitten); ANURAK PONGPATIMET, pp. 20 (purrs), 22 (stalk); Harto Tompel, p. 20 (stalks and pounces); TAMER YILMAZ, p. 20 (licks fur); Life in Pixels, p. 21 (puppy); GeorgePeters, p. 21 (wags tail); artemrybchak, p. 21 (fetches and learn tricks); YAY Media AS / Alamy Stock Photo/ Alamy, p. 21 (gets baths); anetapics, p. 22 (fetch); Nils Jacobi, p. 22 (pounce); Blanscape, p. 22 (snouts).